HANGING LIKE HOPE ON THE EQUINOX

Donna Pucciani

virtual artists collective ☞ 2013

Hanging Like Hope On The Equinox
© 2013 Donna Pucciani
donnapuccianipoet.wordpress.com

VIRTUAL ARTISTS COLLECTIVE
vacpoetry.org
ISBN: 978-0-944048-49-8

Text and cover design by forgetgutenberg.com
Cover photo by Donna Pucciani.

Acknowledgments

The following poems have appeared in various forms in the journals below:

"Aleatory" in *Slant, Gihon River Review;* "Vertigo" in *Summerset Review, Stand;* "Losing the Words" in *Prairie Winds, International Poetry Review, Iodine;* "Post- Operative: Night" in *The Kerf;* "Prayer to Santa Teresa d'Avila" in *Staple, Tribeca;* "To A Friend on the Occasion of His Accident" in *Willow Review;* "Malaise" in *Metamorphoses;* "Waiting for Surgery" in *JAMA;* "Perchance to Dream" in *JAMA;* "I Lost My Car" in *Flint Hills Review;* "Crossing Off the Names" in *Concho River Review, Out of Our;* "Bones" in *Feile-Festa;* "At the Chiropractor's" in *Eureka Literary Magazine, Newport Review;* "In the Dark" in *International Poetry Review;* "Your Side of the Bed" in *Christian Century;* "Seeing Clearly" in *Clark Street Review;* "Old Together" in *JAMA;* "Turbulence" in *Southern California Review, Ambit;* "Palm Sunday" in *Cairn;* "Digit, Avila" in *Atlanta Review;* "Thinking of Death at the Open Rehearsal" in *Istanbul Literary Review;* "Death of a Student" in *JAMA;* "For Anton" in *Tribeca;* "Remembrance" in *Poetry East;* "Ferris Wheel" in *Pulsar Poetry;* "Goodbye to All That" in *Front Range Review;* "Afterlife" in *Front Range Review, Roanoke Review, Staples;* "When I Die" in *JAMA;* "Passing" in *Summerset Review;* "Lost Season" *Caveat Lector;* "Heron on the Roof" in *Bard;* "Hoarfrost" in *Borderlines, New Poetry Appreciation;* "A Fine Snow" in *Pinyon Poetry;* "Icebound" in *Clark Street Review, Bard;* "In winter, dawn" in *New Poetry Appreciation;* "Solstice" in *The Old Red Kimono, Illuminations;* "Meltdown" in *After Hours, Freshwater;* "The First Day of Spring" in *Bluestem;* "From Mud" in *Iodine;* "Blackbird at Dusk" in *Lost Hills Anthology;* "Cardinal Virtues" in *Front Range Review;* "Gone" in *Imagination and Place Anthology;* "Weather" in *America;* "Storm with Fruit" in *Gihon River Review;* "Returning" in *Poetry on the Lake Contest Anthology, Acumen;* "Post-Operative" in *Stand, Down in the Dirt;* "Travellers" in *North 49.*

Thanks to virtual artists collective, especially to Steven Schroeder and Regina Schroeder, for making this book a reality. Thanks also to the Poets' Club of Chicago for their cheerful and unsparing critiques, and to Larry Janowski for his generosity in reading the manuscript. Deepest gratitude to my husband Peter, my constant editor, greatest critic, and truest friend.

For Peter

Contents:

Part I:
FRAGILITY

"And all our yesterdays have lighted fools
the way to dusty death …"
William Shakespeare

Aleatory

There's an order
to the universe, my father said,
and pointed to books on the shelf
that explained everything

except the randomness of things,
the way happiness and sadness
unravel like old socks,
or stars.

Vertigo

You are dizzy again today.

       Your hazel eyes become
                 two different birds, one a fat
     sparrow, the other a bloodshot finch.

          The last two times,
the doctors found nothing.
     Just a brain, we joked.

You return to bed, lie back

          on the pillow that becomes a cloud,
             and wag your head side to side,
     the prescribed exercise.

Someday soon the room will stop

            circling your body like
   a giant bird of prey,

             will land on the blankets,
   enfolding you with white wings,

        still.

Losing the Words

The words were here once.
They have flown miles away,
years into the future,
back into the mouths of many nights,
a deserted shore where the tide
takes days to come in,
dragging driftwood across the sand,
forgotten phrases from a place
where everyone we have loved
is dead. Whole sentences are buried
in furrowed earth, or on a beach
with broken shells like skulls.

Read to me the stories of the young.
I will find the syllables again, make them grow
like Rapunzel's hair, Pinocchio's nose,
or the goose that laid the golden egg
and hatches verbs, throws them
into an August night among the meteors
when nobody is watching.

Can anyone avoid the eventual solitude
of a street without language,
the deserted houses, the speechless windows?
The gibbous moon's hidden slice
is the word I've been searching for.
If you happen to see it, nail it
to the barn door, glue it
to the petal of the rose, taste it
in a ripe tomato, fold it into butterfly wings
that have long since forgotten
the cold coma of the cocoon.

Post-Operative: Night

The night opens before me
like a giant flower, waiting.
I dread the dark.
You will try to stand up in a dream,
lose your balance,
crumple to the floor,
broken pieces of yourself
clattering across the hardwood
like the bones of stars.

I fear sleep,
falling into the mouth of the orchid.
On the lip,
I feed myself to the gods of exhaustion.
They are hungry tonight.

When I hear you stir,
my electric leap sparks to your side.
After the bathroom, I fold you
into bed again among the tired linens,
prop your leg up on planets of pillows,
and orbit you with my love.
I smooth your hair, stroke
your bloated ankle, pull the quilt
to your chin for another hour.

In all our lifetime together,
there was never such a tender place
as the sole of your foot.

Post-Operative

I. Leg

Purple and green
below the newly-stapled flank:

inside, shiny titanium,
a cobalt socket pure as sky.

The knee is lost in a bowl of fluid,
the calf white as a peeled potato

globed and hard, the sockless foot
a bar of soap.

II. Hematoma

Leg ripe to bursting,
gorgeous late-summer melon!

Two days after surgery,
titanium hip-magus

sprays crimson gardenias
on the left thigh.

Fuschia blooms purple,
black orchids with yellow tongues,

the jungle of your sweet blood
a tangle of hot vines.

III. Agitation

Two nights after surgery,
a morbid surprise—

One a.m. it begins,
the dance of the fingers

on torso, face, sheets
tangled, pulled up, cast off.

Luminescent pillows,
a pre-dawn marathon.

I take your hand,
hold it to my cheek,

steady, steady,
blissful immobility

before the nose is rubbed again,
the smooth hair over your brow

patted like a magic lamp,
your hands in perpetual

motion, wielding
a terrible charm.

IV. Swell

Alabaster foot, soapstone calf
moon-carved, blue-veined marble ankle.

Snowdrift piled high on a pillow,
your leg an unknown tender sepulcher,

testament to last week's surgery,
the body's protest in the form of fluids

pooling under tissued skin
mottling at midnight.

V. Milestone

Sun shawls through maple leaves
as if today were special.

The doctor removes the staples
that bind skin-fringes

over artificial bone. Jagged edges
have not yet healed over destiny's teeth.

You wear your scar
like an old soldier, limping

proudly from the hospital
with your newfound cane.

VI. Inheritance

This is my father's walker,
cane, commode, used against

Parkinsonian tremors. We never thought
we'd need such things, bulwark against

the constant test of hip or knee.
Come shine or rain today, the drizzle

of a British countryside, or mere
Mancunian gray over Chicago,

you walk unstitched, lurching
into the path of old age.

You have only a little genie in a cane,
a loyal doglike walker, the throne

of a heavenly commode,
and Papa's voice:

Walk not, like me, trembling into the dark,
but into your brief future sound and fit

to find the dappled spot where
the road ends. Til then,

we travel together, your hand
on my cane.

VII. Unassisted

Today you try to throw away the cane.
You stand on the perilous edge of air,

feeling weight on the new hip,
a metallic guest in an aging body.

You wobble, a precarious debut
for the interior limb, surprised

by instability, and take a step
or two. Hands become flippers

in a sea of carpet, walls, chairs,
your arms wings incapable of flight.

Your Hand

Autumn now, and the sheets are cold,
our flesh shivering
at first encountering the night.

The trees turn a gradual gold
in long-shadowed afternoons,
and suddenly it's dark at five.

We put off bedtime,
cheering ourselves with television's
endless search for criminal intent,

and nod sadly at the nightly news—
wars, the politicians who make them,
children shot dead at school.

Overtaken by fatigue,
we clamber into bed, lie down
on cool linens, knowing that anxiety

will keep you awake. I feel
your warm hand seeking its usual place
on my thigh, and resting there.

Side by side,
we remember your surgery a month ago
when something anesthetic

absconded with your sleep,
and gave instead
a restless wakefulness.

There will be time enough to sleep
when we are dead, we say ironically,
and make a celebration of the night,

your hand my harvest moon,
still bright with that best of all senses,
touch,

beyond sight and sound,
its heat tindering the nocturnal fire
of old love.

Prayer to Santa Teresa d'Avila
for my niece

Cooped up in her apartment in Madrid,
a young woman with an empty stomach
bloats from intestinal terrors fed by bacterium
on stray lettuce or undercooked pig.

She runs to the bathroom
every half hour, filled with sickness
and trying to empty it. Her stomach hurts,
her thigh muscles taut from the wasting.

She has dragged herself to the clinic
three times for powders. When well,
she instructs the doctor in American verbs,
but now she is void of all but exhaustion.

She has put aside her week
teaching English to small children
who sing rhymes in broken Anglo.
They miss their teacher with tights,

boots, tunics, and beads:
Where is Miss Lori?
And she has missed the weekend parties,
lying alone on rumpled sheets.

Santa Teresa, do you remember
the lizards at Burgos? the floods?
the hideous cod-cakes in the hospital?
Do you recall how you had no time

to get sick, with new convents waiting,
ecclesiastical legalities, eccentric monks,
mystical visions? I pray you now,
pass over her

with snow falling from the sky in wonder.
Feed her salted crackers and broth.
Dress her in clean linens.
Turn her darkness into light.

To A Friend
on the Occasion of His Accident

Don't tell me you didn't think about it
as, hungry for life, you shifted Alpine snows,
the sky following you,
sun bronzing your face.

Don't say that when the plane landed
in Hong Kong last month and you disembarked
purposefully with your leather briefcase,
you'd forgotten the turbulence over the sea.

And when, just walking along in Milan,
your heel caught the cobbles and your knee gave way,
turning you suddenly into the curb
as though heaven itself had discarded you
like ash off a cigarette—
don't pretend you didn't feel, for a moment,
when the ligament snapped, the fear of not-being.

And as you wondered, in a microscopic vision
of annihilation, if your last blink
would embrace mountain, cloud, moon,
or a bit of paper on the street,
the gods looked down and sent you pain,
but said, "Not yet."

You lie in bed fingering forty stitches
of surgical thread, watching the emptiness
of your anger float across the ceiling
like a dark bird, but for now,

immobility is a passing shadow
waiting for tennis and sun. Your broken body
will knit itself together for a few more
winters. In fact, you can feel the ligaments mend
as you listen to voices, birdsong, bells.

Malaise

Carmen's cough
is persistent and dry.

Her husband Pasquale
has high blood pressure

and bad digestion.
Her brother in Naples

is riddled with cancer
but walks all over town

with tubes and bags
strapped to each leg

believing still
in the permanence
of earth and sky.

Waiting for Surgery

Tonight the world smells of smoke,
vinegar, rust, ripe pears, ancient herbs,
the spices of chrism.

The moon's thin blade
wants to slice me in half
under the surgeon's hand.

It won't happen for a month.
My belly's field of dimpled flesh,
full and luminescent,

awaits the flash of the knife,
dreaming of itself scooped out,
like autumn's golden gourd.

The moon will curve again,
become the thin smile of scythe,
to savor the wound and its harvest.

So this is how the mind goes,
one fuzzy item at a time,
the lint of life floating through the brain
like so much snow, a certain stillness
at dawn. No need to find the car keys,
grab a coffee to drink on the expressway
in the prison of one's car.

There's plenty of time now to miss the turn
for the grocery while thinking about dinner
or yesterday's chat with a former student,
Dianne something, who wrote a paper
on Melville, used to be a runner, scholarship
to Duke, or was it Northwestern?

It used to be so hard
to empty the mind of committees, meetings,
the colleague who knew everything,
to stagger out of bed in the dark just to write a note—
call so-and-so first thing in the morning—

then to lie back under the covers, waiting
for the anesthetic of sleep, that sweet paralysis
of the mind that now creeps in unbidden
at two in the afternoon when I nod off,
an old copy of *The Stranger* falling from my hands,
the sound of rain breaking a month-long drought
with the remembered scent of ozone.

I Lost My Car

again today.
I'd gone to the grocery
with my usual list
so as not to get home and discover
that I'd forgotten onions or bread.

I thought I'd parked in my spot
opposite the stop sign, that red balloon
that never pops or bobs or floats away,
just waits for me where other cars
line up in diagonal rows.

But today for a moment a void
yawned and swallowed my car.
I hung on to my cart, wandering the lot
with vacant eyes which made a woman
in a grey wool coat glance with pity,
then look away, thinking of yesterday
when she herself had shuffled
outside the hardware store
seeking her black van
in a sea of identicals. My car,

fortunately, is blue and emerges
from the rows of silver look-alikes
with appropriate individuality,
and though my vehicle is small
and plays the hiding game
with its larger cousins, its bluebird
wings are bright enough to flap for me
on a good day when the sun's gone in
and clouds illumine the sky

with the heaviness of snow. And so,
against a world of white and blacktop,
a cerulean song is heard, and I walk
purposefully now, myself again, my car
a car, not a bird, the stop sign
not a balloon but a sign.
I bury momentary terror
under groceries piled in the trunk,
knowing that losing my car
is not really what I fear.

Crossing Off the Names

Funerals of friends are becoming commonplace.
One gets to know all the silent parlors
previously unnoticed while commuting to work
or en route to the store for bread and meat
to stay alive another week, and feeling lucky.

The colors are always neutral,
carpets plushed in soft green
or pale pink like the powdered cheeks
of women who have come to say goodbye.
Paneled walls are hued the warm brown
of fellow golfers who have just
changed from polo shirts to dark suits,
recalling the last time
they all played the course together
and wound up too early at the tenth hole
for Scotch on the rocks.

It used to be that lying stonebound
in a silk-lined box was for the elderly,
a grandparent or dowager aunt.
But now the dead seem younger,
our age. Survivor guilt plagues us,
or shock that they'd outraced us to the Gates.
A vague sadness pervades the parlor
as we shake our heads, murmuring
Too young. Today, a younger colleague
called by cancer, whose only fault
was optimism in the face of doom.
Yesterday, the math teacher at the high school
in the midst of an equation, seeking the value of x,
finding the unknown sooner than expected.

I must remember to cross off the names.
I might forget at Christmas,
sending a disastrous red and gold card,
or mail a birthday joke of sorts. At the coffin,
I stand respectfully, kneel as if to pray,
make small talk, essentially useless,
enduring an odd intimacy with the corpse
and its family of strangers.

I must go now,
deciding to clean out the basement,
or not. A walk in the woods, or perhaps
a phone call to my niece in Spain,
whose name is yet among the living
in the old leatherbound address book.
Her line is busy. Looking out the window
at spring, I am glad of that.

Bones

Dug up behind the church
on top of the mountain
that overlooks the sea

skeletons hide
in a box called an ossuary
that rests somewhere

in church, perhaps
under the stone floor.
The village is haunted

on moonless nights
when even the priest
has doubts about God
and the location of bones.

At the Chiropractor's

We come here to get cracked,
like eggshells, or codes.
We are all on intimate terms
with pain – the neck askew, the hip awry,
the lower back rotated like the globe
of the world that keeps turning,
the shoulder tugging downward into hell.

In the waiting room, we avoid
each others' eyes, read *Business Week*,
pretending to be whole, but even those
who care for others' lame bodies
have fallen prey—the nurse who lifted
one patient too many, the dentist
whose discs finally rebelled against
the music of his drill.

We gather together to peer into the darkness
of our strange, twisted muscles. We will be
called one by one, each to a different cell
to manipulate the misbehavior of sinews
which makes us fully human, and for which
we give thanks.

We can function during the day.
But when no one is looking, we crouch,
then arch at the computer, curl sideways
on a sofa with a handful of pills, curse
the ice pack and the fire in equal measure,
assume strange postures to banish the Furies
from our swiveled spines.

Here is my agony. Where is yours?
Never mind. We hide our misery
behind magazines and smiles, awaiting
the sound of our names, the clipboard

that charts our bodies' tender aches,
the hands that, at least for a moment,
will break us open to the sun.

In the Dark

At the altar, a girl in a cassock
snuffs out the candles one by one.
The long pole with its bell-shaped end
swallows tongues of fire.

The empty nave mourns the end
of light, of flickering warmth
around which seekers have gathered
on this dark Sabbath morning.

Stained glass hears only
the hiss of smoke rising in threadbare wisps.
Flames eat oxygen, borrowing it
from our very breath.

The faithful yawn from lack of air,
a sleepy acknowledgment that
the prayer of light has failed to bring
the splendors of paradise.

But blackened wicks
bless the darkened aisles with little
invisible deaths, an unexpected innocence
retrieved from the chalice of shadows.

Your Side of the Bed

It's time to rotate the mattress.
Your side is well worn
from the gravity of heavy sleep

whereas mine has only the barest
outline, my small frame
pressed into it invisibly—

the tall and the short of us,
the snore and the silence,
the kick and the toss,

the quiet staring into the dark,
blankets and quilts for every season,
the listening for each other's breath

and wondering when sleep
will press the pennies of death
onto eyelids closed for the last time

and then, ever the want of warmth
and the smell of skin, the other's cheek
pillowed inches away.

Seeing Clearly

Now when we kiss
our eyeglasses click.
This is a function of age.
I have become even more nearsighted,
you, farsighted.

You hold me at arm's length,
peering across the silent fires.
I pull you closer, squint into your body
like a spent match.

And now when we touch,
more flesh is felt
as gravity and weight
pull us towards the earth
from which we were made.

The slow, deep lovemaking
finds the point at which we focus,
the middle ground where your sight
touches my own myopic vision,
the moment evening becomes night,
where we find the moon's perspective.

Now when we kiss
our eyeglasses catch,
the sad plastic of old passion
ticking, clicking.

Old Together

Our moments collide
in empty rooms,
long shadows on the walls,
the old-fashioned clock on the bookcase
chiming Westminster.

Most times we ignore each other,
you at your books, I at my verse,
when suddenly ice clatters on the pane,
a train shudders in the distance,
reminding us that we are

here, awake, a still life in yesterday's
cracked bowl, I a bruised apple,
you a yellow pear, our skins touching,
the afternoon light winging over us
like some bright butterfly.

Part II:
TRAVELLERS

"Our revels now are ended…"
—William Shakespeare

Jogger

I fell in love
with a stranger today
a middle-aged man
much younger than I

whose belly and jowls
flapped gently as he ran
searching in vain for youth
and health and that feeling
of flying he barely remembers

Still Life, Twenty-First Century

A music book lies open on the piano.
A hundred years ago,

there would have been a vase of flowers,
fruit in a bowl, or a carafe of wine,

but now only a cup of coffee
half-filled, a pencil stub to mark the score,

a cell phone. Behind,
a muntoned window waits for sound.

An invisible pianist
moves one finger at a time,

in tune with the void.
She rises from the bench,

a wingless butterfly, and lights
on the arm of the sofa,

where a man with no body
waits to touch her.

Travellers

Again, the suitcases brimming
with underwear, electronics,
and the currency of strangers.

After a night over the ocean,
we find other items: toothbrush,
a car for the opposite side of the road.

The years have flown behind us
in the headwinds, our lives flapping
like the wings of sea-birds, or jets.

We land in familiar places,
sleep together under the cool of a window
that opens onto brick houses and sheep.

On television yesterday,
Buddhist monks made a painting
with colored sand, intricate and brilliant.

Temples, birds, trees in blossom.
They'd worked for months. Children of tourists
stood on tiptoe to watch them destroy it

with gentle, deliberate fingers,
their faces tranquil, without regret.
I have tried to pack light,

only one pair of shoes
this time, and no books.

Turbulence

The airplane bobs over the Atlantic
like a cork in a tub. Seatbelt signs
blink mortality, ring innocuous bells

borrowed from Macy's, the old store
on Seventh Avenue with the wooden
escalators. Will my demise

come from impact, frozen waves, or
the shark's bloody muzzle? Anyone knows
these seats are not meant as flotation

devices. Who gets the furniture, the jewelry?
My niece will take the rings, that's certain.
And who will discard the manuscript, not knowing

it is a work of unfathomable brilliance?
Oh, yes: the fathoms. Sorrento, the bay.
sunlit cliffs, cousins, a language of the heart.

On this starless night of dark violence,
only the shaking, the sudden drops, the iced wings,
the juddering, as if the plane is chilled

to the rudders and needs the blanket of day
for warmth, which is only hours away.
One wonders if the pilots were caught napping,

taken by surprise, and when exactly
did the flight crew decide not to serve coffee?
My dinner is lost in my ribs. Plastic chicken,

frozen salad, dead roll and butter.
I'd wanted to live until breakfast. Each bump brings joy,
each swerve sorrow. Marriage in the university chapel,

daddy in the wheelchair, Lori a wrinkled rosebud,
now teaching English in Madrid. I should have
cleaned out the basement. After thirty-odd years,

will we have the unexpected privilege
of going down together? And who
will feed the cat?

Palm Sunday
Northern Spain

In the cathedral at Burgos
a *cordillera* of Baroque altars
tumbles an avalanche of golden saints.
At Santander, we find a hostel,
stroll the gleaming avenue of closed shops,
the harbor, then are caught
in a procession of red-robed choristers,
priests vested in penitential purple,
white-garbed children bearing flags
amid boisterous drums and cathedral bells.

Hoisted on the dais, a painted Christ
rides a donkey. Everyone waves
armfuls of palms, waiting for Jesus
to wave back from Jerusalem,
to give them a sign of what is to come.
They have been told
that he goes to dinner and death,
the same as they. Nobody asks why,
but their singing is hypnotic, mystical,
lifting them up to the lowering sky.

Digit, Avila

The finger of Santa Teresa
points brown and delicate,
cut from her right hand
for viewing by the faithful,
its small gold ring set with
a square blue jewel, its fingernail
growing small hairs like whiskers.

The plain glass vial
clouds with five hundred years
of piety. Models of her castanets
click silently in the next case.

Today, Easter Sunday, we recall
not her stigmata but her ecstasies,
a foretaste of resurrection.

Once, with Juan de la Cruz,
Teresa levitated while discussing
the Trinity. Both clutched their seats
and felt themselves lifted,
chairs and all, by the hand
of the Almighty. Pointless
to resist His will.

We leave the museum,
not sure if the tapping we hear
emanates from the soles of our shoes,
the mahogany castanets under glass,
or the ring clacking in the reliquary.

Train Station, Berlin

He returned today from Prague,
where he'd put his mother's ashes
into the river. His face in the revolving
door is whole and solid,
not yet fragmented.

He rushes now after noticing
that the sky is the same color
as when he left, the hue
of the dark river, the gray
bearing down on him.

He'd had insufficient patience
for the scattering, dumped
the contents all at once,
some sinking, others riding
the tide in random clumps.

Now he returns to the office,
the place of the living,
must report to his cubicle,
check a thousand flashes of information.

Running for a taxi, he looks forward to
his intimate relationship with
money. He left his wife years
ago, pays someone to do his
laundry. He never wonders when next
someone will kiss him on the lips.

After work he'll unpack, head
for the gym where he sweats
He has forgotten the scent of apples,
his children's arms.

His odyssey is mapped on
his cell phone. He glances
to the left. This is the accident
we call life. Today the train
has run its course. The view in winter
will be different yet the same.

From the corner of his eye
he sees a dog wagging
what used to be a tail.
He stops to pocket his passport,
looks back. A wet stain
spreads on the pavement,
smelling of death.

This has been a short trip.
Purposeful. Now he is surrounded
by students with backpacks.
No women in sight. They are
home baking bread. He is
caught in a cage of sunlight,
blinded between the iron bars
of shadowed slats. He prefers
the dark.

He cannot locate his life
in the unyielding geometry
of tracks. After all these years,
he thinks of her pale hand
on the butter dish, the wan sun
in the mornings, the egg yolk
broken in the frypan.

He checks his wristwatch,
given by his father, unfashionable,
still ticking. His heart beats
like the untold tale of autumn,
without pulse, without blood.

But yes, he can move his feet, his arms,
his suitcase on wheels, must
keep moving like the sun igniting
the steel beams of the station,
where God hides behind a girder
in the mythology of strength, light
glancing off His tired, luminous face.

Why I Like La Boheme

The characters are artists, poets.
They burn furniture for warmth.
They eat little, drink wine.

Their makeup runs under the lights.
They sing in theatrical rags
as though each aria were their last.

Cafes fill with friends
and philosophy.
A stranger helps a neighbor

find her key. I feel cold all over
during the snow scene,
for I've seen this opera so many times

I can smell its body under the coat.
A serrated song cuts my torso
into pieces of sad flesh as a blot

of spotlit Mimi blurs. Her man
burns under the English translation.
I close my eyes and remember

what love is like—
a small rain under my ribs,
the moon over Central Park,

bookcases made of wine crates
in a sixth-floor walkup, a window
balancing burglar bars,

roach powder on the stairs.
Essentially clownlike, Rodolfo
calls out at the end for the woman

who has died, although this opera
is not the one about the clown.
He cries as the curtain descends,

soaking the applause in misery.
The audience is happy to be sad,
but in life—

they are sad to be happy,
a kind of survivor guilt
while holding hands under the stars

or kissing beneath the elevated train
that rumbles away, leaving only
a spark of moon in its wake.

Thinking of Death at the Open Rehearsal
The Chicago Symphony Orchestra

Where music meets the morning,
keyboard and fingertips connect
like sunlight on steel.
Uchida plays Mozart.

For the seventh day my cousin Greg
is no more. A scant week ago
he walked Rufus on a beach in Maine
as though it were any other day, but not
the day of sudden extinction. A tightening
on the treadmill at sixty-three.

The pianist hugs the first violinist
before the soaring begins.
What is it like to be a pile of flesh,
the bird that fell from the nest
or hit the glass in full flight?

Uchida conducts from the piano, her hands
clawing the air, pulling sound from strings,
the notes a mere vibration
played a second ago by fingers and breath.

Now her arm lifts as if holding Mozart
like a fallen sparrow, cuing flutes for the minuet.
Someday the players, now alive and strong
in their wood, brass and silver,
will play a final cadenza, rosin the bow
one last time, wipe metal keys with a soft
white cloth, replace the instrument
in its velvet-lined box, shut the lid,
snap the clasp.

If there's time, they will
sing themselves to sleep. If not,
like Greg, they will be surprised by flight,
the last movement, as always, allegro.

Greg, you are where the sound goes,
where the vibrations are felt along the hairs
of a cellist's arms, where a bird sings its last
in the deep green pines.

A bit less stringent, Uchida says.
Play with a smile, with a little more joy.

Demise

Finches flash their yellow with surprising frequency
in this coolest of summers, borrowing a cup of sunlight
for feathers, slices of lemon for wings, a patch
of black velvet for a cap.

Just as one nester scallops between ash and elm,
lacing in miniscule dives, its lamppost perch
signaling fires at dawn, another becomes
a sidewalk heap of ochre the size of a hand,
drawing an iridescent chorus of flies, leaking
almost no blood, but bearing witness to the predations
of some neighborhood cat who made a game of her,
a fallen angel caught in the solitude of flight.

Nameless friend, you can never come back.
There's no way to remember you—no stone, hymn,
or urn, just the mausoleum of this sad world
that is poorer now without your beak, claw,
and olive eye, your song from the butterfly bush,
your reflection in the periwinkle lake
quickening the morning. Only the sunflowers
sing the echo of your yellow, only the harvest moon
brims with golden promises before smothering
in its own shroud of black silk.

Death of a Student

After the concert, she'd swallowed
a pink pill embossed with a daisy
and chased it with beer. Some say
rat poison was the secret ingredient.
The ambulance elbowed through traffic
while her brain swelled like a toy balloon
and coma turned to death in a white room.

No medical miracles for a teenager
in flip-flop shoes and short skirts.
She'd planned a major in psychology
at a state university, but the call of Ecstasy,
like the song of Sirens, brought her
crashing to the rock. No harps, no hymns.

Was the crow on the cradle
the day she was born?
Her body at the wake looks pasted
on satin pillows like a paper doll,
or a collage of sawdust and lace,
the powdered visage of mortality.
The crisis team from the high school
filters through the crowd.

Chatter circles like random birds
through the funeral parlor, where flocks
of the distraught huddle at the coffin
or squint at photos and verse. Her poems
talk of teddy bears and jewelry,
her grandfather's chew-tobacco,
grapes bunched together for survival.

Life sifts quiet as sand through fingers,
formless as an egg slipping through a cracked shell.
Two girls enter in sunglasses, their cheeks wet.
I hug them, touch their faces, glad they are alive,
their arms warm and golden.

And so this dark summer begins and ends
with a white coffin borne by a limo
to the city of headstones, lowered into earth
amid the groans of ropes and relatives
and the fierce tremolo of adolescent regret.

For Anton

I've always loved Chekhov,
the manic visitations, the incessant
comings and goings.

I've never had to abandon a villa
or watch an orchard fall to the axe.
But I have known the languid whistle

of a train in the night,
its trestled lullaby rocking over water.
I have counted the miles of roads,

overnight stops
at inns blinking parts of neon words,
and a Marx Brothers kind of madness,

the way people and ideas hang mid-air
like a juggler's fruit, the slapstick entrance,
the bored exit. I know

Vanya's melancholy,
having hoarded the same sense of loss,
pacing the empty rooms of the mind,

leaning on my stick of nostalgia.
I follow in the footsteps of the three sisters,
their vague sadness interrupting my nights,

and the sea gulls circling.
It's only make believe, my father said of books
when I was four, but he was wrong.

The loneliness of snow is unmatched, bitter,
a new goodbye every minute. Farewell,
this day and its little disappointments.

Farewell to the colleague who died young,
the parent who fought the extended tortures
of old age. Farewell to the lovers, their sad beds,

and the cactus that blooms once a year.
You knew all the partings, Anton, the openings of doors
and the closings.

Remembrance

Today I write a poem for you, Papa.
Not a sad poem, for we are finished with sadness,
you and I. No more wheelchairs. The tremors
have ceased, spasms calmed on a cloud.

Hallucinations have ascended the pink
institutional walls into the scent
of autumn. Your shoulders
took the shape of wings.

Birdsong, rain, and lightning
erase your long loneliness. The cries
of the demented have borne you into heaven,
where you will smile with your eyebrows,
resume your funny little walk,
and call me from above your sugar plum.

Ferris Wheel
Navy Pier, Chicago

Jump on, don't hesitate.
Follow the fat man
who's slow sliding out of his seat,
dazed from light and space.
Follow his wife, who shuffles behind,
her gray hair showing patches
of pink scalp when the wind puffs,
her arm reaching for his.

How long have they been married?
They have just been to heaven and back,
like birds, falling stars, or the sunlight
that slants through the spokes like pickup-sticks,
twigs of fire burning white over the lake.

They concern themselves with bunions and buses
and whether the roast has defrosted for dinner.
The wheel holds the shape of their eyes,
the form of gold rings on swollen fingers,
the wide-brimmed hat she wears in the garden,
the vinyl records he plays in the basement on rainy days,
or the hub caps he collects in the garage.

They have paid six dollars apiece
to dangle high above the lake,
not thinking of the roundness of their lives,
the arc of their tired love.
They recall the carnival in Little Italy fifty years ago,
where, in the grip of creaking metal,
they floated above the tenements in Lower Manhattan,
saw Lady Liberty, green and ever young,

wave at the Circle Line, flaunting her spiked crown. They have come full circle.

Step up. Swing into the shafted sunlight.

somewhere in Chicago

a piano plays
in a rented room
where the roof does not leak tonight

outside
a man with a dog
pauses to listen

loneliness lights a match

Goodbye to All That

A certain stillness
pervades the snow today.
Tired from restless drifting,
a docile powder becomes
its new identity, no longer shifting
but quiet in its acceptance of melt,
the decay that comes to weather events
and all living things—the dried leaf,
the overblown bloom dispersing its last pollen,
the nest of the flown robin.

This quietness knows in itself
the futility of further movement,
and I am reminded of my spouse's jocund words
as I approach the dentist's chair,
or mine to him before the surgeon's knife:
Lie back and think of England.

Now, when whole countries fold
into decomposition, and only the rich survive,
I think briefly to ski today across the frozen fields,
then observe prairie grasses sticking through
what yesterday was mounded white.
Our revels now are ended.
Nowhere to go, nothing to do
but watch the melt.

Afterlife

And then there's the question
of what happens to the bulbs
underground, curled up below
the earth like oversize snails,
becoming brown and brittle
after a life in yellow dresses.

They have drowsed to the rocking
cradle of wind and leaf, felt
the dried bones of prairie grasses,
heard the flame of the cardinal
in the Norway maple. By All Souls Day,
they burrow down into the first snow
under the sleeping pines.

I want to be buried in yellow silk.
My body will turn brown, my limbs
shrink into little knobs of ash.
But my shroud will not fray or fade.
Dyed in a vat of sunlight,
it has already come from worms
eating their mulberry lunch
while I was walking up the long hill,
reading the *Paradiso*,
or writing a letter to Spain.

Vanishing Act

Piece by piece
we will leave this spinning planet,
exit when we least expect it,
when gravity is napping
and death is paying attention.

Unfair
there is no choice of when,
what disease or random act of violence
will pierce the aura of ourselves,
bursting it suddenly like a pricked balloon,
or letting the air out by inches,
moaning like a banshee in a swamp.

No point in guessing
when fingers will fly off like gulls
into the sun, or when feet will detach
and paddle into the sea, wearing only
the fatigue of pavement, corridor and hill.

Legs will follow,
the quivering thighs of invisible lovers
grasping what is no longer available.
Then the arms, waving like ferns in the shadows,
disappear into the trees for one last embrace.

The torso eats itself whole
the way Mount Snowdon swallows a cloud.
The last to go is the head –
ears listening in vain for the flutes of reprieve,
mouth kissing the void of remembered affection
or muttering a prayer of false comfort,
nose sniffing seashore, ozone, perfume, bread,

eyes witnessing the loss of everything—
sun for you, moon for me, the little planet
of our house, a favorite pair of shoes,
the skyline of our city etched on the lake,
one last book. Finally, the heart
explodes like a meteor shower,
the stars dying of love.

When I Die

When I die, let it not be winter
sifting me into ash, the bitter ice
making me colder than extinction,
the ground too hard
to take my body into its arms,
the sky too heavy for my soul.

Let it not be spring, when grass
awakens, trees and all good things
smell of the earth, my bedfellow,
making me jealous of blossom, bird
and seedlings waiting to burst.

Let it not be summer, friend of bees
and butterflies, baseball and picnics.
How could I bear to leave the soft nights
with their long hair blowing,
the lights of glowworms and stars?

Let it be autumn, when evening
lifts like a curtain, revealing
the last dance of zinnias, the curve
of spiked lavender like arched eyebrows,
Russian sage trembling like f-holes
in the body of a violin.

In autumn, may death surprise me
as I prepare for winter, store garden tools
in the garage, exchange cotton for wool,
listen for the heater's low rattle,
put the kettle on for tea.

In autumn, death will feel
like steam rising from the grass
on the first cool day, when trees
bend and swoon in unsuspecting winds
and the soil is still warm and shivering,
waiting for me.

Passing

You bring the coffee to my desk,
leave it silently at my elbow

so as not to disturb the thoughts
which the hours have finally yielded.

Your wordless visit,
wrapped in the texture of silence,

settles on the back of my chair,
one sleeve swinging from

the old sweater hanging there,
your receding footsteps

a mute canto dedicated
to the passing of the years.

Part III:
WINTER'S LEASE

"…and summer's lease hath all too short a date."
—William Shakespeare

Lost Season

Trees leaped orange today
where mere blue looked on, windstruck.
The lawn shone green and tangerine.

Autumn has deplaned.
Gold exhales brown. The peacock summer
spills into the fox's den.

Soon grey-veined winter will burrow
into the violet heart of things,
camouflaged behind the shed

filled with garden tools. The ground
smells cold as an airport floor.
Jet fuel gathers in the throats of those

checking schedules, watches, cases.
One entire season has vanished
in a month's absence. Homecoming

witnesses the work of the wind
gathering up the gold, sugaring
the cold vague aura of the moon.

Heron on the Roof

Still as Buddha, across the backyards
a feathered clump hunkers on the tiles,
headless.

The great blue I've seen
standing on stilts at the water's edge
has flown aloft, settled into its cloud-body,

head tucked under wings,
the way we look when we get old:
a grey bulk, a loss of grace.

No movement from the gutter's edge,
the silent soffits warmed twice this week,
seen from the opposite bedroom window.

I wait for it to unfold
from its bundle of down, to balance
on stilts, stretch its neck.

I imagine a brush painting
inked on a pale sky, and on the chimney,
a white fan opening.

Hoarfrost

A harsh welcome for the unsuspecting dawn,
precursor of snow. The hint of death

we've all been waiting for. The moon
dusts the earth with the seductive breath of illusion.

The good life has hummed into daylight,
stoic after the long night's black largo,

but not for long. The hoarfrost comes
like a floater in the gray-blue eye of death,

a song with no guitar. That was yesterday.
We didn't know how lucky we were.

Now snow piles up in heaps, a canticle
to an alien god from the monophony of ivory sky.

Black Ice

glosses dun twigs
with false romance, threads ill-fated
desire through a glitter of trees,

draws the riddle of water
from an ice-bound sky, crushes
the fog that shrouds the deer in the wood,

stills the hand of a lover on a warm thigh
with the miniscule clatter of a thousand
fingernails drumming on the table of earth,

sabotages trucks on the highway,
their cabs askew, cargo awry, blocking
three lanes, and cars with brake lights red

skate sideways down the white line's sheen
the moment a transparent sadness
turns evil, the spectacle of white

winter now ebony sliced thin
by star-blades in the flip of a coin.
The dark shows through.

Hapless pedestrians face themselves
in the sudden mirror of night,
brought to their knees, cracked, shattered,

felled by a speck of sleet multiplied
to the hundredth power,
eye to eye with the earth

that will take them back some day
after the sprained wrist, the broken leg
has healed.

A Fine Snow

Snow started again,
those little stinging flakes
that make the whole world
soft, vulnerable.

Like past sins or wounded love,
tiny crystals shatter the night
when least expected.
Not harmful, we think,
coming en masse from a dead sky.
Painting the trees in pointillistic ice,
they surprise us with their regrettable
tenacity, the cruel dazzle of a million
pinpricks, later, even broken bones.

Boots, coats and hats, the woolly
appurtenances of protection,
cannot save us. Even when
we close our eyes,
small pieces of sadness
stick to collar, eyelash, and cheek,
cashmere and sackcloth,
a wintry pollen of discarded pain,
the shredded fabric
of an unremembered past.

Icebound

The aching earth stands speechless overnight,
when every living thing is packaged
in the hard darkness of ice.
People miss their own weddings.
Even funerals have been cancelled,
the ground inaccessible.

Still, corner shops are doing a record business.
Red double-decker buses are rocking
around bends carrying the bundled bodies
of the exhausted. Children sled downhill
in colored scarves. Later today their mittens
will dry on radiators all over Britain,
their miniature Wellingtons dripping
in homes smelling of fish and chips.

Airports are closed again today. Another train
sits broken in the Channel tunnel.
The whole world creaks, and Liverpool
is running out of salt.

In winter, dawn

is the best time for thinking
and watching the sad strings of lights

blink blue on the snow, the hills
a darker shade of grey than sky,

the pink-dusted sun blessing
a horizon of dying holidays.

The cats on the sill stare lidless,
guarding the houses. And we,

recalling days and decades
when we'd have been up for hours

shoveling snow, driving sideways
down the street, slowing

but not stopping for red lights
in the frozen foggery of waking.

No longer the need for telephones,
computers, crowds, documents

at six a.m. Now is the time
for coffee, newspapers, a poem or two,

kisses leftover from the night,
the touching more important

than whether the sun will rise today.

Solstice

The shortest day of the year
genuflects on snow-dusted sidewalks,
its frozen fingers folded in prayer,
its head bowed in the overwhelming darkness
beyond the fringes of dead leaves
and the inaudible sighs of the moon.

This day wants to remember lilacs,
the acid taste of backyard tomatoes
climbing their tilted cages,
the sweaty cries of children
playing baseball in the street.
The lengthening nights have dimmed
all such remembrances, have closed the eyes
on the corpse of summer with leftover pennies.

No full-bodied tides of memory
will wash the pale face of this brief daylight hour,
but only a dampened corner of nostalgia
like the hem of a handkerchief
from Auntie Agnes' purse, scented with
some antique London perfume, her bony fingers
lifted in a last wave.

The snows of February will bring
the light again, padding softly
in old socks towards March's new green,
April's yellow. By May the days
might even pray to apple blossom
and viburnum.

Meltdown
from a photograph by X Woods

I never heard the crack.
I never saw the first fissure
as the temperature rose above freezing
for the first time in months.

The clods of ice wander
listlessly on dark industrial waters
like lost sheep. They watch each other
decay in the oil-slick river,
then swallow the poison themselves,
tokens of their own disappearance.

Once they were whole,
a wool-white vestiture
that clothed the river edge to edge,
the seamless fabric of winter's sorrowful loom,
unmoved and unmoving, draped
like the bedclothes of a dying woman
for whom hospice cannot patch together
another life, whose fingers pluck
the linens in brief spasms.

The frozen anti-shroud unravels
day by toxic day
as thaw brings certain death.
Now the flock of chunks
has morphed into unrecognizable shapes.
Say your prayers, little lambs.
Join the jigsaw river.

The First Day of Spring

A pale sun surfaces
in the tidal pool of sky.

Light! The pearl
has eaten the oyster.

The earth smells of old apples
and of things dead or a long time dying.

Oaks watch the tips of daffodils
making the cracked earth smile.

It has been a cold winter
and I am exhausted by hope.

Two robins are feathering
and beaking on the lawn,

between frolic and panic
at the first clap of thunder—

isn't this the way all lovers feel
in the early blush of nakedness?

Tendrils of rain
uncurl in the shelter of danger,

while a grove of pines sways,
the sap rising.

From Mud

If you have ever watched
the candles in a little wooden church
lit one by one by a small girl
in a white cassock, you know
that wisdom begins with the mystery
of wick and match and child.

In spring, from turgid earth
that has been frozen so long
it does not even know itself
and has become hard-hearted
to shivering beasts like us,
the first small crocuses lip their way
in centimeters of palest purple
from tips first brown, then green.
They open the way mouths
prepare to kiss, or wax becomes flame.

Light, touch, and early bud
are created anew. The days lengthen
out of the darkness, gradually boots
are changed for sandals,
and the million sadnesses
burn down to wisps of smoke
that hang like hope on the equinox.

Blackbirds at Dusk

And so they come again this evening
to settle together in their favorite tree,
fifty or maybe twice that number,
the same black wings and yellow beaks
that lined the telephone wires last night
outside the hardware store, facing
the headwinds off the farmer's field,
watching the silo turn orange
in the dying light.

They have discovered the last country road,
the final stretch of field to horizon
in a land of big-box stores and parking lots,
the meeting places of humans.
They create their own city without walls,
money or vehicles, without worry about
marriage and divorce, kids, and doctors,
knowing only twig, seed, and worm,
not knowing when death will make a hundred
into ninety-nine, a gospel of the unafraid,
chattering, then stilled.

Now they huddle together,
talking of earth and rain,
whether it will be a good year for corn.
In the wind, which turns cold in late afternoon,
their iridescent ghosts remind us
that their conversation is untranslatable,
their love for berries and bark incomprehensible
from my late-spring window.

The fragility of lace on sky
veils a concert of small chatter, shrieking silhouettes,
a new definition of melancholy, of saying goodbye,
companionship without invitation, government,
neighborhood, marriage, or class, only
a favorite branch, wings, the sky, each other,
a convention of claw and wing
in one particular random tree.

Cardinal Virtues

On the top branch of the tallest ash
sings a wild strawberry

in the form of a bird—
cheer-cheer-cheer-cheer-cheer—

the descending arc falls to earth,
echoes on this blind winter day

when the neighbors are at work
or minding the children

or drinking a first desperate coffee.
This treebound drop of blood

glistens on a gray sky,
and like a clock ticking

or the sea somewhere
surrendering its tides

to the moon's need,
another, more subtle voice,

the color of burnt berries,
becomes a living weathervane

in the mirth of morning,
opening her beak to him.

Gone

The storm blew in when we least expected it.
An early darkness swiveled the leaves
in purple silence. When the lights flickered,
a sudden rush of rain framed the still life
of tree on car.

The adjuster has come to figure the damage.
He stands in the empty space of remembered buds
and incipient fruit. The shattered windshield
webs its way across the car, spidering
in the arms of a dented roof.

We hadn't known the pear was dead inside.
It had even bloomed this spring, arching over
the driveway in white waves, denying the inevitable.
Now the core is mulch for other trees,
or logs for a neighbor's winter fire— useful at least.
But no chance for us to say goodbye.

Storms are again forecast but cannot hurt
the downed Bradford, now a diaspora of chips
and firewood, a victim of its own softness,
black rot having gnawed its way between branches
that had held each other much too close.

Weather

Tonight thunder hangs on the sky
like God's underbelly.

We soon forget the deep rubbings
of crickets in the scorched night

and God becomes kabuki
in a white mask, her performance

crackling over the hushed audience
of earth. Lightning cloaks

the black bones of night,
fastens the hidden folds of stars.

The night my father died, I'd watched
for storms, some cosmic reflection

of his demise, this human being
of gigantic proportions, now unscripted,

consigned to the wings, insensible body
shrouded in sheets of electric white.

But no tempest, just tropical heat
in the wrong hemisphere,

mute claustrophobia, little wooden
flutes of humidity.

Storm, with Fruit

The basket of fruit brims
in the shadows. By tomorrow the heat
will be leaking the juices of a peach.

Storms roll in from the south,
and warnings blink by the minute,
tracking a plum-blood sky.

That first electric flash
splits past from present,
lighting the violence of time.

My father died ten years ago today.
I'd seen him just a week before,
a shriveled apple in a wheelchair.

On the tentative shelter
of the porch, I sit on a rocker,
peach in one hand, crossword in the other.

In the ball of blackening sky
I watch the horizon
fashion his eyes, two ripe stars
glowing.

Two squirrels

chased each other this morning
when the humid air
awaited snow

up and down and swiveling
around the only oak on the block
they flew pointed nose to the

other's tail (such a little reddish
snout) arrested this moment only
the unblinking eye of one

seeking the grey fluff
of the other not even a breath
but listening for the claw

on brown bark clicking
hearing without seeing
imagining acorns

or summer or bells
so grateful that the other
is there even if

on the other side of the tree
or in the black crotch thinking
of other yes even if hidden or
hiding

Returning

The little fireflies of dreams
have disappeared. They were
proof of God in the summer dusk.

They have turned to snowflakes
or the cold dots of stars
so that dreams, or gods, might survive,

returning to earth in fingerprints of light,
a letter from an old friend decades gone,
meteors with their long hair flying.

Donna Pucciani was born in Washington, D.C., grew up in New Jersey, graduated *magna cum laude* from Marywood University with a degree in music, and earned an M.A. and Ph.D. in Humanities from New York University. She taught in secondary schools and colleges in the East and Midwest for several decades before retiring to write full-time.

Her poems have been published on four continents, translated into Chinese, Italian and Japanese, and nominated several times for the Puschcart Prize. She has won awards from the Illinois Arts Council, the National Federation of State Poetry Societies, Poetry on the Lake, and Chicago Poets and Patrons, among others. A resident of Chicago and Manchester (England), she served for many years as Vice-President of the Poets' Club of Chicago.

Pucciani's previous books of poetry include *The Other Side of Thunder* (Flarestack Poetry, England 2006); *Jumping Off the Train* (Orchard House Press, Washington State 2007); *Chasing the Saints* (Virtual Artists Collective, Chicago 2008) *To Sip Darjeeling at Dawn* (Virtual Artists Collective, 2011); and *Imperfetto* (Blue Forge Press, 2013).

.

CPSIA information can be obtained at www.ICGtesting.com
Printed in the USA
LVOW06s0519031113

359782LV00004B/157/P